All About Your Rabbit

Cont

Rabbits have been domesticated for over 2,000 yea[rs], reared for their meat and fur. The Romans kept them in special walled enclosures called leporia. It was only in the late 19th century that we started to keep them as pets.

This book is aimed at the new owner of a rabbit who wants to find out how to care for their pet, and for those who already own one or more rabbits but would like to know more about them.

Is the rabbit a suitable pet for you?

Rabbits are now the most popular of all the small pet mammals. They have many advantages as far as the pet owner is concerned, including:-

- Low cost to purchase and maintain.
- Quiet.
- Hardy, and able to survive in suitable outdoor housing.

However, there are some disadvantages:-

- Low cost to purchase and maintain.
- Quiet.
- Hardy, and able to survive in suitable outdoor housing.

No, you're not seeing double! The very same characteristics that make rabbits such good pets also mean that they are very common[ly] neglected. Why is that?

Because rabbits are inexpensive to buy, there is a temptation to ta[ke] them on as pets without thinking carefully about the care and attention that they will need throughout their lives. Because they ar[e] quiet and can be kept outdoors, it is all too easy to forget about the[m], particularly during the dark and cold winter months, at a time whe[n] they need more care rather than less.

A pet rabbit is a sensitive and feeling animal, and unlike a toy, it cannot be discarded once the initial excitement of a new present has worn off. So do think really carefully about the long-term responsibilities involved before you take one on.

Remember, rabbits move pretty quickly and can bite and scratch quite badly, and so they are not ideal pets for young children, unless they are very closely supervised by an adult at all times.

Many of the small mammals kept as children's pets – such as hamsters and guinea pigs – are rodents, but rabbits are members of a different group of mammals called lagomorphs. A major difference is that the rabbit has two pairs of upper incisor (gnawing) teeth (although the second pair are very small), compared to the single pair that rodents possess. Like rodents these teeth keep growing throughout life, and are kept chisel-sharp and at the correct length by the top and bottom sets wearing against each other.

The enzymes that most animals have in their small intestines to digest food cannot break down the tough cellulose that comprises a large proportion of the coarse vegetable matter that rabbits eat. To get over this problem, the large bowel (the lower part of the intestines) is well-developed, and contains many special bacteria to digest the food.

Most of the digested food is passed in the faeces at night, and these special, lighter-coloured stools have to be re-eaten by the rabbit in the morning so that the digested nutrients can be absorbed from the small intestine a second time. So if you see your rabbit eating its faeces for breakfast, its habits are not really disgusting as they may seem.

Most reputable pet shops sell rabbits and the best will advise you on which type to buy. Otherwise you may know someone locally who breeds rabbits and possibly competes at rabbit shows. Such a breeder would be able to give you all the advice you need. You might be able to find an address of a local rabbit club from your library or pet shop. You may also be able to acquire a rabbit from a friend that has bred some, or you can make inquiries at reputable pet shop.

In all instances, look for a rabbit that is clean and well cared-for. In a pet shop, it is a good sign if the staff are knowledgeable and can give advice when you are making your choice. Resist the temptation to buy a sickly rabbit just because you feel sorry for it – you could end up with a lot of heartache, trouble and expense trying to get it well. Select a young rabbit, at around six weeks of age, so that it grows up accustomed to plenty of handling and human contact.

Look for a clean, well cared-for rabbit that appears lively and alert.

One rabbit ... or two?

It is nice to have more than one pet housed together to keep each other company, but rabbits do not alwa

get on well together. This i especially true the case of two male (buck) rabbits. They w almost always fight once they are sexually mature, and ca inflict serious injuries on eac other in the confines of a hutch.

A male and a female will generally get on like a house on fire, but they will produce lots and lots more rabbits unless steps are taken to prevent it.

Some people advocate keeping a rabbit and a guinea pig together, but guinea pigs are very timid and can easily be bullied by a rabbit. A female of one of the smaller breeds of rabbits would generally be the best choice to house with a guinea pig, but they must be introduced to each other at an early age and supervised closely.

Generally, rabbits do not always get on well, particularly if you try to house two buck rabbits together.

The signs of a healthy rabbit

A healthy rabbit should be alert and active during the daylight hours. Look for the following signs of good health:

CONDITION: overed and ed. No nal swellings.

BREATHING: Quiet and regular. Should not be laboured.

EARS: Ear flaps undamaged. No discharge or redness in the ear canals.

EYES: Bright and clear, without any discharge

NOSE: Clean and free of discharge.

T: Well-groomed. Should e soiled or matted, cially around the rear.

MOUTH: Incisors should not be overgrown. Dribbling can be a sign of problems.

Rabbits are easily frightened and must be handled firmly but gently. They will occasionally bite, and will often inflict painful scratches by kicking out with their powerful legs. Rabbits should never be picked up by their ears. The best method is to grasp their ears and the scruff at the base of the ears with one hand, while the other arm cradles the rabbits legs. If necessary, tuck the legs into your body to prevent kicking.

Rabbits should be transported in a top-opening cat carrier. You may need to put a light towel over a very nervous rabbit to calm it down so that it can be lifted out. If a rabbit needs to be restrained for examination or some other minor procedure it will become passive if held on its back. If the ears and scruff are held in one hand, the rabbit can be turned over. With large rabbits, the hind legs can be controlled by tucking them under the arm of the same side, leaving the other hand free. If the rabbit is spoken to quietly, stroked under the chin, it becomes almost hypnotised and can be easily handled.

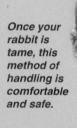

Once your rabbit is tame, this method of handling is comfortable and safe.

An Indoor Pet?

More and more people are realising that you don't have to keep rabbits outdoors – they can make very fine indoor pets. Rabbits tend to use one area of their living quarters as a toilet area, so once you work out where that spot is, they will generally oblige if you put a litter tray on that spot. Of course, they should still have a hutch, where they can be kept out of harm's way at certain times.

The main problem with indoor rabbits is their tendency to chew things that they should not. For this reason, it is best to limit the rabbit to areas where they cannot do too much damage, and particularly where there are not any electric cables that they can get at. Providing your rabbit with plenty of safe chewing material will help.

DID YOU KNOW?

Lagomorphs such as the rabbit are more closely related to hoofed animals such as horses than to rodents.

Rabbit Breeds

All breeds of pet rabbit have been bred from the one species of European Wild Rabbit, but there are now more than 50 breeds and about 80 varieties in a wide range of sizes, colours and coat types.

These range of types are divided into four main groups:

Normal Fur

Including breeds such as the Chinchilla, Havana, New Zealand and Fox.

Rex

This type has a short, velvety coat about an inch long, and includes the Self, Shad and Tan.

Satin (below): Rabbits belonging to this group have a flat, shiny coat.

Normal fur: Havana.

Satin

This type has a very flat, shiny coat in a wide range of colours such as Argent, Himalayan and Opal.

Fancy Breed

Includes the long-coated Angora, the big-eared Lop and the tiny Netherland Dwarf.

Rabbit Breeds

DID YOU KNOW?

The heaviest breed of rabbits are Flemish Giants, which regularly reach 11.3kg, (almost 25 pounds). In 1980 a five-month-old French Lop doe was weighed in at a Spanish show at 12kg, over 26 pounds. The heaviest recorded wild rabbit was a mere 3.74kg, or 8 pounds 4 ounces, compared to an average of just 1.58kg.

The Best Pet Breeds

Here are just a few breeds of rabbit that make good pets:

Angora

Probably bred here in the 17th century, th Angora can yield up to 1kg of wool a yea That's great if you're into knitting, but remember that all that dense, fluffy coat needs regular attention to prevent matting

The Chinchilla: An attractive silver colour.

▲ *Impressive coat,
but the Angora needs
a lot of regular care
to keep it looking
like this.*

Chinchilla

With an attractive coat colour
that resembles that of the small
rodent with the same name, they
used to be bred for their fur, but
are now deservedly popular as
pets.

Rabbit Breeds

Dutch

One of the most popular breeds kept today. They were originally bred for their meat, but their relatively small size (around 5lbs, or 2kg, body weight) and their lively nature, make them excellent pets.

Himalayan

These have a white body and distinctive dark 'points', rather like a Siamese cat. They are quite large rabbits, but generally have a very placid nature and are good with children.

...ops

...here are several
...rieties of lop rabbits, all
...ith the distinctive 'Dumbo' ears.
...e dwarf lop is probably the most
...itable as a pet, as it is generally
...ciable, and not too large.

...etherland Dwarf

...ry popular as a children's pet
...cause of its small size,
...eighing only about 2 pounds
...kg). They require less living
...ace than the larger breeds,
...t are not as sturdy and can
...metimes be a little nervy. A
...aller pet is not necessarily the
...st choice for a smaller person.

Size
Your rabbit will appreciate spacious living quarters, so buy the biggest hutch you can afford. If you keep more than one rabbit, or one of the bigger breeds, more space will be needed.

Sleeping compartment with solid front ●

Well-insulated and sturdy construction ●——

An outdoor hutch will need to be more sturdily constructed than one for indoor use. It should be made of marine plywood or hardwood suitably treated (but not on the inside). Waterproof roofing felt should be fitted to the top, sloping to the back, with an overhang at the front.

There should be two compartments divided by a partition with a sliding door. The larger compartment should have a wire-mesh front, and the smaller sleeping compartment should have a solid front to help keep the warmth in. Cleaning is easier if the compartments have removable metal or plastic litter trays that can be slid out from the bottom of the hutch.

● **Raised off the grou**

The hutch should be rai at least nine inches off ground on legs to prev dampness permeating. If attached to a run, a ra will be needed so the rab can get in and of the hu

Warmth

There is no need to provide extra heating even in winter, but it is essential that the hutch is waterproof and well-insulated. Some heavy sacking on top of the cage will provide extra insulation, which can be pulled down over the front of the cage at night.

Living quarters with wire-mesh front

The wire mesh on the front of the cage needs to be fine enough to exclude rats and mice from entering. The opening front panels must be secure when closed to prevent the rabbit from escaping, and to stop foxes from breaking in.

Bedding material

Rabbits produce a lot of urine and faeces, so the cage will need cleaning every couple of days, with a more thorough spring clean about once a week. Provide your rabbit with plenty of clean and dry bedding material. Wood shavings, straw or peat all make a good base, and rabbits do appreciate some hay, which can be eaten as well as being used for bedding.

Make sure you purchase hay or straw from a reputable source, and check to make sure it is clean, free from mould and not excessively dusty. Shredded paper is also available from pet supply stores, and this is a relatively mess-free alternative for indoor rabbits.

DID YOU KNOW?

Some lengths of fairly wide drain piping are often appreciated in a rabbit's run, which can be placed together to make a maze. This will provide shade, and cater for the rabbit's instinct to live in tunnels.

Other Equipment

FEEDING BOWL:

A ceramic bowl will be needed for dry food. This should be deep enough to keep the food clean and dry.

WATER BOTTLE:

Water bottles with a valve on the spout at the bottom, which can be turned upside down, are most commonly used nowadays as they keep the water cleaner than in a bowl. Ensure a supply of fresh water is always available, and check that the bottle does not leak water on to the bedding. In the depths of winter you must check outdoor hutches regularly in case the water in the bottle has frozen.

Fresh water should always be available.

Run, Rabbit, Run...

n outdoor run will decrease
e risk of rabbits escaping from
e garden, and it will also stop
em from nibbling at highly-
ized, or even poisonous,
ants. The rabbits will be safe
d secure, protected from
edators, and they
ould be fairly easy
catch at night.
A simple run
n be

nstructed from a softwood
mework covered with wire
esh, taking great care to
sure there are no sharp ends
otruding that could harm the
bit. If you cover one end of
e run with some translucent
astic, this will provide a
aded area, otherwise the run
ist be sited so that natural

shade is provided on sunny
days. Of course, the rabbits
will need a water supply within
the run.

As rabbits can dig very well,
the run will be more secure if it
has a wire-mesh base that is
coarse enough to enable the
rabbit to nibble at the grass
underneath easily. The run can
be moved around the lawn to
give the rabbit new areas to
graze on, and to avoid
damage to the grass. Do
not allow a rabbit that
has been over-
wintered on
hay to

suddenly have
unlimited access to fresh
spring grass. Too much grass,
eaten too quickly, may cause
diarrhoea.

Even if your rabbit is allowed
freedom indoors, it will benefit
from access to an outdoor run
when possible.

Rabbits will eat a wide variety of

vegetable matter, but it is best to base their diet upon a balanced food, such as that formulated in pellets for laboratory rabbits.

Many rabbits do very well on a complete food based on alfalfa. They enjoy hay, especially in winter, when they do not have access to fresh grass and boredom can be a problem. Lettuce has very little nutritional value, and too much can cause diarrhoea, but sprouts, cabbage, carrots, cauliflower, peas (and their pods), swede and turnip are all appreciated.

Resist the temptation to save money by buying prepared foods in large quantities if you only have one or two rabbits. If the food is stored for too long it may lose some of its goodness, or it may go off – especially in damp conditions.

Wholemeal bread that has been dried in the oven until hard will help to exercise your rabbit's teeth.

DID YOU KNOW?

The rabbit's mouth contains 17,000 taste buds, compared to 10,000 in humans.

DID YOU KNOW?

Three rabbits will eat as much grass in a day as one sheep, making them a serious pest to farmers. Ferrets were bred from polecats to go down burrows and kill rabbits, but in some coastal regions crabs and lobsters were sent down burrows to try and chase them out.

Dried food can be left in a bowl in the hutch for the rabbits to help themselves. However, succulent food must be removed from the hutch before it goes off.

bles such as
e will be
ated

Breeding

Sexing Rabbits

Female rabbits are called does and males are called bucks. It is very easy to tell them apart as adults: the doe has a slit-like vaginal opening, whereas the buck has very obvious testicles, and the penis can be exposed by pulling back gently on the genital opening.

Sexing young rabbits is more difficult – even experts sometimes get it wrong! It is best to compare a male and a female side by side to see the difference. In the doe the vaginal opening is more noticeably slit-like, and in the buck, there is greater distance from the anus to the genital opening. Although the testicles do not descend until the rabbit matures sexually, it is still possible to expose the penis in a young rabbit.

Family Planning for Rabbits

This is pretty important if you want to keep mixed-sex groups of rabbits together. Even if you allow your rabbits to breed, this must be limited as you will not be able to cope with the vast number of young that will be produced. Uncontrolled breeding is also likely to have an adverse effect on the does, resulting in a loss of condition.

Modern anaesthetics are now much safer than they used to be, and although it must be accepted that rabbits are higher-risk patients than dogs and cats, surgical neutering is a viable option. Castration of male rabbits has been used for a long time to help reduce the aggressive tendencies that some bucks develop as they mature, but it is also possible to remove the ovaries and womb of female rabbits, just as in cats and dogs.

Doe rabbits can breed at any time of the year, as their ovaries produce ggs 'to order', as a result of the act of ating with a buck. They can have several ters each year, with an average of five per ter, but it is not advisable to allow a pet e to have more than three litters a year. he doe should be taken to the buck to see if e is ready to mate.

Pregnancy lasts about one month, and the egnant doe will make a nest, lined with her vn hair, ready for her litter. She will preciate a shallow nesting box about 2 ches (6cm) deep, lined with hay, in one rner of her sleeping compartment.

The young are generally born at night, and oblems are rare. The doe should be atched from a distance, and veterinary sistance sought if she strains for more than hour without producing any young.

reat care must be taken not to distress the e or to handle her young before they erge from the nest, as she may turn on em and kill them.

t is normal for her to eat e afterbirths, which is pelled after each by.

Although the young are born very immature, they develop quickly:

Day 7
Fur growing

Day 10
Eyes open

Day 12
Ears open

Day 18
Leave the nest and eat solid food

Day 60 (2 mths)
Fully weaned and independent

Day 150 (5 mths)
Sexually mature and able to breed

 # Caring For Your Rabbit

Grooming

The amount of grooming you rabbit requires will depend if i is longhaired or shorthaired Shorthaired rabbits do not nee regular grooming, but whe they are in heavy moult usually once or twice a year they will benefit from bein brushed. A longcoated rabbi such as a Cashmere Lop, wi need grooming on a weekl basis, while the Angora need thorough grooming severa times a week

Nails

Many rabbits go through their lives without ever needing their nails clipped, keeping them worn down by digging and hopping around on hard ground. However, if the nails are overgrowing, they can be cut back with nail-clippers to about ⅕ of an inch (½ cm) from the end of the quick. It is easy to see where the pink, sensitive quick is in unpigmented nails, but this may be harder when the nails are coloured. If a nail breaks accidentally or is cut too short, it may bleed profusely. This is uncomfortable for the rabbit, but there is no need to panic as the bleeding soon stops.

Teeth

It is not unusual for a rabbit's teeth to get too long. It occurs if the teeth grow out of alignment and fail to wear against each other properly. This can cause a lot of a discomfort, with the rabbit showing difficulty in eating, and possibly dribbling saliva down its chin. It is quite easy to see if the front teeth are overgrown and a vet can cut them back. But overgrown back teeth are more difficult to see because the rabbit's mouth is small. A vet can use an lighted speculum to see the back teeth. If they need filing down this will have to be done under anaesthetic.

Vaccinations

Rabbits should be vaccinated against myxomatosis and viral haemorrhagic disease, both serious viral diseases that are usually fatal. As myxomatosis is spread by biting insects, even a rabbit that lives on its own can contract the disease. The vaccinations need boosting at least once a year, and this is a good opportunity for a regular health check.

Going Away

Rabbits should not be left alone for long periods. If they are safely locked in a clean hutch, with a supply of dry food and water, they should be fine for a couple of days. If you leave your rabbit for a longer period, try boarding it with a vet, a pet shop or perhaps a breeder. If you have a good neighbour, a check once or twice a day for feeding and cleaning should be sufficient. Make sure that whoever looks after your rabbit knows all about its needs, and leave a number for your vet in case of problems.

Health Problems

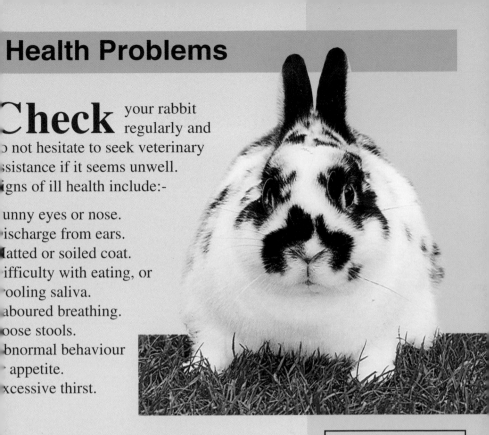

Check your rabbit regularly and do not hesitate to seek veterinary assistance if it seems unwell. Signs of ill health include:-

runny eyes or nose.
Discharge from ears.
Matted or soiled coat.
Difficulty with eating, or drooling saliva.
Laboured breathing.
Loose stools.
Abnormal behaviour
 appetite.
Excessive thirst.

Common Ailments

Snuffles ●————————

Respiratory infections are common in rabbits, especially if their housing is poorly ventilated. They can cause 'snuffles' with a chronically snotty nose and noisy breathing. Although antibiotics can sometimes upset the natural balance of bacteria in the rabbit's bowel, this is a situation where they generally have to be used.

DID YOU KNOW?

The sense of smell is very important to a rabbit. It is used for seeking out food, sensing the approach of predators, and for identifying their territory. Male rabbits mark out their territory by spraying urine, and by transferring scent from special glands under their chin on to their paws, and then stamping it along the borders of their patch.

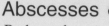

Health Problems

Abscesses

Perhaps the most common problem of all in rabbits are abscesses filled with a thick, toothpasty pus, caused by an organism called Pastuerella. Small abscesses can be lanced and treated with antibiotics, but rabbits often get multiple ones that fail to respond to treatment.

Heatstroke

Rabbits are much more susceptible to the effects of excessive heat than from the cold. Make sure your rabbits have adequate shade in the summer and plenty of water to drink. If your rabbit seems weak or collapsed, and you think heatstroke may be the cause, sponge it down with cool water immediately to reduce its body temperature, and then see veterinary help.

Fly Strike

All too often a consequence of diarrhoea, will quickly gain a hold in hot weather wh the skin is inflamed and soiled. Eggs are on the hairs, and the maggots that hatch o will eat into the flesh of the rabbit. This n prompt treatment by a vet if the rabbit is t saved. Good hygiene and regular examina of the rear area of the rabbit can prevent t problem.

DID YOU KNOW?

Rabbits are colour blind, but with their eyes set high up on either side of their head, they are able to see about 300 degrees of the full 360 degrees around them. In this way they can spot any predator stalking up behind them while they are grazing.

Diarrhoea

ommonly due to infections or parasitic
roblems, or sometimes simply a dietary
roblem. Providing a complete dry food
nd removing greenstuffs from the diet
ay do the trick in mild cases. Laboratory
nalysis of a faeces sample may be needed
establish the diagnosis.

Fur Balls

air balls can build up in the stomach,
ausing a loss of appetite and distension of
e abdomen. A 5ml dose of liquid
araffin (mineral oil) may clear the
roblem, but sometimes surgical
tervention is needed.

Poisoning

nenome, autumn crocus, bluebells, elder,
gwort, foxglove, poppy, nightshades and
ild clematis are all examples of plants
at can be poisonous to rabbits. There are
specific antidotes to most poisonous
ants, but, obviously, restrict access
any you think could be
oublesome. Rabbits are
nerally pretty sensible about
hat they choose to eat, but if
u rabbit is off-colour, develops
arrhoea, twitches, or even has
nvulsions, you should seek veterinary
vice. Take along samples of any suspect
ants your rabbit may have eaten.

IF your rabbit is seriously unwell, your veterinary surgeon must be contacted without delay for assistance. In this case, a responsible adult will need to take the rabbit to the surgery and authorise any treatment that may be needed.

Most small animal veterinary practices see a large number of small mammals and are very willing and able to treat them. Nowadays it is not uncommon to anaesthetise rabbits in order to carry out surgical operations such as tumour removal or draining large abscesses, although the risks are greater than for a cat or a dog undergoing a similar procedure.

The most important care for a sick or injured rabbit is to keep it warm and administer fluids to try and prevent dehydration, which can occur quite quickly. A dropper or a small syringe is ideal for administering solutions, but do not use excessive force, and remember that they can do more harm than good if fluids are inhaled.

Commercial rehydration powders that are designed to be made up with water can be purchased from a vet or a chemist, but a rabbit will only take a few drops at a time. Alternatively, you can use boiled tap-water

hat has been allowed to cool, adding a heaped
ablespoonful of glucose powder and a level
easpoonful of salt.

Small wounds

mall wounds can be gently flushed with warm water
nd treated with a mild antiseptic, but any major
njuries will require veterinary attention. Keep a suitable
arrying box to hand, as you never know when you
may need one at short notice.
A top-opening cat
carrier is ideal.